MARENZIO

Oxford Studies of Composers

General Editor : Colin Mason

Egon Wellesz: FUX
Denis Arnold: MARENZIO
Basil Deane: CHERUBINI

Oxford Studies of Composers (2)

MARENZIO

DENIS ARNOLD

London

OXFORD UNIVERSITY PRESS

NEW YORK   TORONTO

1965

Oxford University Press, Amen House, London E.C.4

GLASGOW NEW YORK TORONTO MELBOURNE WELLINGTON
BOMBAY CALCUTTA MADRAS KARACHI LAHORE DACCA
CAPE TOWN SALISBURY NAIROBI IBADAN
KUALA LUMPUR HONG KONG

Grateful acknowledgement is due to Faber & Faber Ltd. and W. W. Norton Inc. for permission to quote translations from Oliver Strunk, Source Readings in Music History

*Printed in Great Britain
by W. & J. Mackay & Co. Ltd.
Chatham, Kent*

PREFATORY NOTE

MARENZIO is the Schubert of the madrigal. Both were masters of setting words to music; both were composers of great charm; and both developed a vein of serious melancholy which gave their later music a new profundity. But whereas Schubert's life and music are fully documented in a vast scholarly and popular literature, it is a measure of our still widespread ignorance of the sixteenth century that Marenzio's music is not available in anything approaching a complete form in modern editions, and that only two really knowledgeable studies of his music exist in any language. One of these, Hans Engel's *Luca Marenzio* (Florence, 1956) is a thorough examination of documents and music which provides the basis for any future monograph on the composer, but is too concerned with bibliography to make attractive reading. The wonderful chapter in Alfred Einstein's *The Italian Madrigal* (Princeton, 1948) is another matter. Written with enthusiasm and an unparalleled command of both musical and literary background, it throws new light on Marenzio's music at every re-reading. Its only disadvantage is that it presupposes an interest and knowledge of Italian literature which few music students possess, and will always be difficult to read without at least an outline knowledge of the work of Guarini, Sannazaro, and Petrarch.

The present short monograph attempts to remedy this situation, and is written for those who have a musical knowledge of the madrigal but lack any skill in the Italian language. Where, as for example with *Dolorosi martir*, an English translation of the period follows the original verse in sufficient detail, I have discussed the English version as though it were the original; and if this may seem to lead to minor inaccuracies, at least it has the virtue of bringing the emotional life of the madrigal into strong focus. The background material concerning patrons and contemporary composers is necessarily less complete than can be found in Einstein, but gives clues to changes in style and spiritual development.

Editions of Marenzio's music are still few and far between. Einstein's attempt at a complete edition, in the *Publikationen älterer Musik* (Leipzig, 1929), went only as far as the first six books of five-part madrigals. Since then two small but worthwhile anthologies have appeared in Italy. L. Virgili's *Madrigali a 4 e 5 voci* (Rome, 1952) contains six madrigals, but in transposed and somewhat unscholarly versions; Mompellio's *Madrigali a cinque e a sei voci* (Milan, 1953) is more accurate and contains some of the later masterpieces. The most readily available collection for the English singer is the useful set of the madrigals published in *Musica Transalpina* in the edition of Alec Harman (London, 1953 ff.), but unfortunately these do not print the Italian text alongside the English. Lionel Benson's editions in the Oriana series are exemplary in this respect, using sixteenth- and seventeenth-century translations where possible, but always giving the original verse. I have referred to madrigals available in these editions and a few others easily obtainable, rather than analyse those obtainable only in the nowadays rare publications of Einstein and Torchi. In spite of this, many transcriptions have had to be made afresh, and most of the later examples have been made from the original madrigal books. For a grant to enable me to do this, I must thank the Queen's University of Belfast. And I must not forget the hospitality and great kindness of Contessa Nicoletta Piccolomini during my stay in Rome.

THE MUSIC OF MARENZIO

I

WE know little enough about Marenzio's life, but the facts, though sparse and apparently unrevealing, are significant enough to act as a guide to his musical style and perhaps to his spiritual development. The surviving documents may be formal, and contain no hint of psychological attitudes, but at least they tell us where Marenzio was born, worked, and died. This, in sixteenth-century Italy, was important. Italy was then no centralized State with a common capital city and a common tongue. It was a huddle of small princedoms and duchies, each with its own atmosphere and culture, its own life and needs, and sometimes even a dialect so strange that it could almost be a separate language. Each had its own poets and musicians, who, according to the interests of prince and duke, were sometimes merely local figures, at other times men of international renown. But since the interests of prince or duke were paramount, even the most famous of poets and musicians were rarely able to escape the influence of their patrons. At the peak of their fame it was impossible for them to transcend entirely this localized culture. Places and patrons were significant facts indeed in the life of the sixteenth-century artist.

Coccaglio, where Marenzio was born in 1553 or 1554, was far from a princely court, and no patron was nearer than Brescia, where for the musician it could be at best the local cathedral. There, half a dozen singing-men, the boys of the choir school, and, on festive occasions, the local *piffari*, or town band, provided the only music the populace could expect to hear. The master of the choristers at the time was a purely local celebrity, called Giovanni Contino, and it is usually assumed that he was Marenzio's first teacher. If so, Marenzio was hardly at the centre of things, and yet, in a way, Brescia was not a bad place for a musician to learn his trade. The courts where real progress in establishing a modern idiom was made were not too distant. Mantua and Parma were both distinguished centres of music-making; Venice was the home of the principal publishing houses in Europe; Verona, nearer still, had its Accademia Filarmonica, which was the most interesting of the purely musical study groups of the time; and Ferrara had taken the lead in the 1550s in producing experimental music, mainly concerned with the possible uses of chromaticism. This activity meant that composers in all the main towns of northern Italy were alive to new developments, and even those from Brescia and its surroundings were kept fully aware of new events. Bearing this in mind, it is surprising that we hear nothing of Marenzio until he was in his mid-twenties. Only in 1577 did he publish some madrigals in a minor Venetian anthology, and only three years later than this did he find a patron to support him.

The patron, hardly surprisingly, was a north Italian prince, Cardinal Luigi d'Este, whose family were the ruling house of Ferrara. The fact that he was a cardinal, although Marenzio was never employed as a church musician, need not surprise us, for just as the Archbishops of Salzburg could employ Mozart and his father, so in the sixteenth century the princes of the Roman Catholic Church had secular musicians to entertain them in their palaces. What is a little unexpected is that Marenzio, who seems to have had no ambitions to be a composer of religious music, should have gone to Rome, for Rome was predominantly a centre of church musicians. Its great composers were the choirmasters and singers of the Sistine Chapel, the Cappella Giulia, S. Giovanni in Lateran, and other distinguished churches of the city. Though they wrote madrigals, this was a side-line for them. They contributed a few numbers to anthologies, and published an occasional madrigal book, but compared with the Venetian or Ferrarese composers, their production remained extremely small. Palestrina's three books of madrigals are dwarfed by the vast numbers of his motets and masses; Giovanelli, Nanino, the Anerios together scarcely composed as much secular music as did Andrea Gabrieli alone.

Why, then, was Marenzio brought to Rome? The answer probably is that there was a great deal of amateur music-making in the noble houses. When Vincenzo Giustiniani looked back on his youth in 1628 he bemoaned the fact that 'in the present course of our age music is not much in use, not being practised in Rome by gentlemen, nor do they sing together with several voices as in past years, notwithstanding that it would provide the best possible means to unify and sustain evening parties.'[1]

Indeed, the very nature of the Roman madrigal indicates that it was designed for amateur singers, at a time when in the north of Italy the composer was ostensibly writing for the virtuoso court singer. Like the English madrigal (which borrowed much of its idiom from Rome), the madrigals of Palestrina and the rest are for the most part in a lighter vein. Even in the last two decades of the century, when passion-

[1] Giustiniani, *Discorso sopra la musica*, trans. by Carol MacClintock, *Musica Disciplina*, xv (1961), p. 220.

ate and neurotic poetry became the fashionable choice of the madrigalists, the Roman composers remained faithful to the scenes depicting the not-too-serious loving of Phillida and Cloris. Their music echoes this make-believe atmosphere in every way. To help the singer, it is on the whole quite diatonic. No one need understand the old apparatus of the modes to sing Giovanelli's *Che poi tu farmi Amore.*

EX I

(And my pain will end)

The melodic lines never make strenuous demands on breath or skill, as on the whole they consist of short motifs and phrases, repeated again and again, to assist the memory. Gone is the virility of rhythm which makes some of the works of Lassus and the Venetians difficult to master. Instead, phrases are neatly balanced, rhythms simplified and regular. And when moments of passion require astringency, dissonance is kept severely under control. Nanino's tinge of the gentlest discord in *De Vaghe Perle* is as far as most Romans will go, although the words suggest a harsher note.

EX II

(Ah, how my heart is slain)

Exceptionally, Zoilo remembers Cipriano de Rore's madrigal *Crudele acerba inexorabil morte* when he becomes agonized,

EX III

(O ever bitter day)

but even here the harmony is logical and of no great difficulty. Compared with the experimental chromaticism and dissonances of several northern composers,[2] it is innocuous. But the cardinal test of the old-fashionedness of these composers is to be found in their attitude to word-painting. All the writers of treatises and practising madrigalists elsewhere agreed on one thing: the music must be joined to the words in a meaningful way. Zarlino, the great influence on all sixteenth-century theorists, had given the basic instructions in his *Istituzioni armoniche* in 1555:

. . . cheerful harmonies and swift rhythms must be used for cheerful matters, and for sad matters, sad harmonies and slow rhythms, so that all may be done fittingly. The musician, therefore, should be warned to accompany, so far as he can, every word in such a manner that when it denotes severity, harshness, cruelty, bitterness and other such things, the harmony should be like this also —that is, to some extent harsh and hard, yet not so greatly as to offend. Similarly, when any word expresses complaint, grief, affliction, sighs, tears and so on, let the harmony be full of sadness. Which will be best done, if the desire is to express those effects first mentioned, by making use of those intervals of the scale which proceed in their movement without the semitone, such as the tone, the major third and major sixth or thirteenth above the lowest note of the harmony, which in their nature are somewhat hard; also they can be accompanied by the suspended fourth or eleventh above the bass, when the movement is rather slow, in which case the suspended seventh also may be used. But when the later mentioned effects are to be expressed, then let the composer use movements which involve the semitone, the minor third and so on, often using minor sixths or thirteenths above the bass, which in their nature are smooth and sweet. . . .[3]

By the time Marenzio arrived in Rome these views were twenty-five years old and commonplace. Discussion had turned to their refinement, and gradually composers had evolved a whole language of conventional images with which to make the words more vivid and meaningful. The idea of height in such words as heaven, sky, ascending and so on, naturally called for an ascending figure; and the opposite, of course, for depth. A sigh was usually expressed by a rest immediately before the word, a picturesque and realistic effect. The idea of darkness, blackness or night often achieved its natural expression in 'black notation'— either the use of crotchets and quavers, or the filled-in semibreves and minims which still survived from earlier centuries, although now

[2] As for instance in Luzzaschi's *Quivi sospiri*, printed in Einstein, *The Golden Age of the Madrigal* (New York, 1942), which was written at least several years earlier than Zoilo's madrigal.
[3] Zarlino, *Tutte le opere* (Venice, 1589), pp. 439 f.

4

commonly used only in the notation of triple time. This was a symbol more perceptible to the singer reading the printed page than to the listener, and so was the expression of the word 'eyes' by two semibreves on the same note. Rarely has there been so detailed a relationship between words and music as in the work of the madrigalists of the later sixteenth century.

But in Rome, the church musicians ignored these methods, or, at their most up to date, used them without enthusiasm. In setting the Ordinary of the Mass, and in motet composition, an abstract, contrapuntal approach was predominant. The general mood of the words would be considered and expressed; detailed pictorialism was rare. In the madrigal the Roman composers scarcely changed this attitude. In part, they ignored the problem by the verse they chose for setting. A great deal of this is abstract and lacks the concrete imagery which was so much a part of the madrigalian poetry used by the Venetians; and when pictorialism does seem to be called for, it is kept to a minimum. Palestrina's most famous madrigal *Vestiva i colli* is a setting of a pastoral scene not unlike Monteverdi's *Ecco mormorar l'onde*, yet while Monteverdi found in almost every line of the verse inspiration for word-painting, Palestrina ignored the words so completely that his madrigal could almost be an instrumental composition. No other composer could write a dissonance to express the word 'soavement' (sweetly), or be completely consonant where the lover's heart is wrung ('Mi stinse il cor'). But Palestrina's interest is clearly in the musical pattern, for he repeats musical sections to different words, in the manner of a French chanson, something which the madrigalists of the 1570s found increasingly abhorrent. Nor were Nanino, Giovanelli, and the Anerios very different at this time. The lady in Nanino's *Porche'l mio amor* slays her lover by her cruelty—in a perfectly pure and innocent phrase without any astringency. When the lover still finds it in his heart to wish her well, the composer manages to put the melisma not on the emotional word 'lieta' (happy) but on 'dunque' (therefore), something which would have seemed incredibly clumsy to Andrea Gabrieli and most minor northern composers.

EX IV

vi - ve - te dun - - - que lie - ta.

It is an understatement to say that these composers were behind the times; they were living in another world. When Marenzio burst into it his success was almost assured from the start by the lack of up-to-date competition. His first book came out in 1580. Two more followed within a year, yet another in 1582. After a pause, 1584 produced three madrigal books and a volume of villanelle. A year later the presses gave light to two more madrigal books, a book of motets and two slighter collections of villanelle. This is the work of a man at the height of his powers; and the number of reprints of these books (not to mention individual numbers from them) shows that his public knew this. Within five years he had become one of the two or three leading madrigalists of his day.

What were the roots of such popularity? The answer can be found in the very first book Marenzio published. Its fourteen madrigals shows a sheer musicality and skill which hardly another opus 1 of the time achieved, and a mixture of old and new which is judicious enough to provide pleasure for practically every taste. For the Roman amateur, there is the same diatonicism, the same shortness of phrase and gentleness of rhythm that Nanino and the Anerios offered him. Although the verse tells of the usual vicissitudes of pastoral love, the mood is for the most part playful, even in the provision of one of those absurd punning echo pieces which were coming into vogue at this time. But if these things were conventional, the actual sureness of touch was not. Few composers show the ability to expand a phrase to give it adequate weight such as we find at the beginning of *Ohime, dov'e'l mio ben*, with the full harmonization of the opening motif at the fifth bar, and the changing of perfect cadence to one of transition at the end of the section.

EX V

(Alas, where is my love, where is my heart)

A quotation from the cantus alone at the close of the madrigal shows how a motif can be given different endings, to create the mood with

6

sufficient intensity while yet remaining memorable for the singer.

EX VI

Che mi-ni - stro mi fai del - la mia mor - te, che mi-ni - stro mi fai

Che mi-ni - stro mi fai del - la mia mor - te.

(Oh cruel fate that brings about my death)

This dexterity comes less from contrapuntal skill than from manipulation of texture. Most Roman composers in developing a phrase were content if they could arrange a contrast between upper and lower voices, with harmony and even the melodies repeated with the minimum of necessary adjustments. Marenzio is rarely satisfied with such elementary methods. A mere glance at one of the most distinguished numbers of the set, *Liquide perle*,[4] shows the range of his resource. The opening section is a contrapuntal passage based on a chanson motif such as Palestrina often used. Marenzio splits the motif into two short phrases (each two bars long) and works both into a marvellous continuity which extends for a dozen bars. He starts with one voice, adds a second, a third, and the fourth in quick succession; but although the bass is kept in reserve for the first climax, and no new material is brought in, the permutations of voice and motif seem endless. When the bass enters the mood changes—and so does the texture, now homophonic and gently dissonant, as befits the lover's sufferings. The homophony is concluded by his sighs which again are left to the upper voices. Then, when tragedy is out of place and he must give more animation, Marenzio returns to contrapuntal writing, and works out a conventional tag by twists of harmony and changes of vocal combinations, while saving the final phrase of the poem for a conclusion which is justly abrupt and tinged with discord, as the lover goes to his death.

Liquide perle is a delight to the musician, and its musical resource made it famous in Italy, Germany, and England (where it appeared in the first book of *Musica Transalpina*). Even so, the real significance of this first volume lies in its modernity, the more especially in Marenzio's treatment of the words. In this he shows himself a true disciple of Zarlino. Very often musical considerations are so strong that we scarcely notice the pictorialisms. Nevertheless they are there. In *Ohime, dov'e'l mio ben* the musical structure is predominant, but there is still the

4 Modern reprints include one edited by Karl Geiringer (New York, 1939) and one with English words only) edited by Alec Harman (London, 1956).

opportunity to express the word 'blindness' in black notation, though this demands a sudden change into triple time. In *Madonna, mia gentil ringratio Amore* the lover finds paradise in his beloved, not unexpectedly with a rising phrase.

EX VII

go - de - rejl pa-ra-di - so, go - de - rejl para -   -   di - so.

'Dolore' naturally produces dissonance, 'dolcezza' clarity of harmony. Sighs are usually preceded by rests. These are all reminders that Marenzio had come from northern Italy; and in one or two madrigals his incipient modernity comes out still more strongly. The most remarkable of these is the miniature cycle setting *Tirsi morir volea*.[5] Guarini's poem, at this time new to musicians, was to become one of the most popular verses for composers, largely because its erotic imagery (with the sexual act thinly disguised by the words 'death' and 'dying') suggests a constant ebb and flow of emotional tension which suits the musician's purpose extremely well. Marenzio's reaction to it is to abandon counterpoint and to write a virtual cantata in which short phrases and sudden changes of texture mirror its fluctuating intensities. There are few places where the voices imitate one another; there is little dissonance, and that little is not at all unconventional. But by the construction of motifs which now hurry on the narrative, and now delay it, Marenzio gives a perfect picture of the act of love. There were to be more spectacular and more highly powered settings of the following words, but no composer conveys more vividly the hastening desire of Cloris, and the tantalizing way her beloved heightens it, than Marenzio in his constant delays of cadence and his refusal to complete the phrase.

EX VIII

Mo - ri cor mi - o   ch'io mo - ro, ch'io mo -   -   ro.

(Die my love that I might die)

The other really modern madrigal in this set is also its most famous number, *Dolorosi martir*. The translation of the verse used by Nicholas

---

[5] The dialogue by Morley, *Phyllis, I fain would die now* (reprinted in *The English Madrigal School*, iv), uses a poem very similar to Guarini's, if rather more innocent.

Yonge in the second volume of *Musica Transalpina* at once shows the possibilities.

> Dolorous mournefull cares, ruthles tormenting
> Hatefull guyues, cursed bonds, sharpest enduraunce,
> Wherein both nights and dayes my hart euer renting
> Wretch I beewaile my lost delight and pleasaunce,
> Woefull loud cryes, sadde scriches, howling lamenting,
> Watry teares shedding and euerlasting greiuance
> These are my dainties and my daiely feding,
> And my liues comfort, bitter gall exceeding.

Its plethora of emotional words, the very continuity of its intensity, were surely the stuff for which the modernist must have sought. There are, it is true, no obvious Zarlinian pictorialisms to be used, but there are no neutral or narrative phrases such as would suit a Palestrina. Every word counts, and Marenzio wrings the ultimate in emotion out of them. The madrigal starts with a slow movement and gradually adds dissonance upon dissonance. 'Night' and 'day' provide a sudden contrast in motion; 'delight', a dancing measure which departs as suddenly as it arrives. The 'loud cryes' are expressed by leaps of sevenths (unheard of in Rome at this time). The difference between 'liues comfort' and 'bitter gall' is pointed by both change of motion and the contrast of sweet consonance and suspensions. Not an idea is allowed to pass without musical expression, and yet, although the madrigal is tightly wrought, there is a sense of expansiveness which delights the singer. Many a later composer was to use the same means to express the words. Few of them would have expressed the word 'enduraunce' so naturally by means of a sequential phrase which is so singable and musical as this:

EX IX

Pictorialism, passion, and a purity of musicianship mingle together in the madrigals of the next five years. In some books one or other seems to predominate, as though Marenzio was catering for several kinds of patron or amateur singer; but in general the tone is the same, with the pastoral hedonism of the Arcadian tradition as the main theme. The lightest touch is to be found in the book of four-part madrigals which was published in 1585. Its very nature—for four-voiced madrigals were by this time unusual for composers following the north Italian style—was determined by the needs of Roman amateurs, and the mélange of pictorialism and singable melody ensured the success which has persisted to the present day (they are still the most reprinted of Marenzio's works). For this book Marenzio chooses verse which has a great deal of concrete imagery. Petrarch's sonnet *Zeffiro torna* is typical in this, its springtime mood expressed in terms of green fields, rejoicing animals, singing birds, and flowering bushes. The composer takes every suggestion at its face value. The flowers flourish with a little melisma: the smiling fields make the singer's lips part into a smile, too, with melismatic scale passages; the birds sing mellifluously in thirds and sixths. There is a touch of anguish as the lover is tormented by his aching heart, and Marenzio naturally turns to suspensions to express it. But the anguish is not exaggerated into tragedy, as in Monteverdi's later setting. Pastoral love, even in its sorrows, is a gentle thing to Marenzio. Feeling is kept under strict control. This madrigal is not only expressive; it is a joy to the singer. Its diatonic vocal lines and short phrases fit exactly the restricted capacities of the amateur, but Marenzio never shows any sign of his restriction. *Zeffiro torna* appears to be built on a broad scale, and is quite large enough for an extended poem because Marenzio knows exactly which phrases he must repeat and which have enough emotional content without development. When he feels repetition to be necessary he finds the same resource as made *Liquide perle* such a success. The climax of the madrigal comes near its second part, where Petrarch can find no comfort in the birds and trees:

> She, she is gone! All that e'er pleased before
> Adieu! ye birds, ye flowers, ye fields, that charm no more.

The first statement of Marenzio's setting uses a series of close imitations between three voices, the tenor being left free to add its own material.

EX X
(a)

When it recurs the tenor is not allowed such freedom. The texture is made taut by his intervention, and the lover's agony is intensified by this. There is no exaggerated dissonance, the angularity of the lines and the cluster of imitative points make all clear.

(everything now seems a desert . . .)

Zeffiro torna is longer than most of the madrigals of this book, but in its balance of gentle pathos and gaiety it is typical. Even where Marenzio chooses verse which might be taken tragically, his music avoids extremes. *Chi vuol udir*, for example, could easily begin with a heavily emotional section, with its emphasis on the sighs and bitter weeping of the poet. Marenzio merely expresses the general mood of the first line by a slow movement with a climactic, though not particularly astringent, dissonance. Then he turns to a happier phrase which is given more development and thus more emphasis. In *Dissi l'amata* (which delighted Hawkins enough for him to reprint it in his *History*) the lover's threat to die at her disdain is never taken too seriously. It is simply a playful conceit of pastoral love, and in the pure diatonic lines and the rest before 'Yes, I shall die' there is no more than a hint of desire, the pleasing pain well known to Arcadian shepherds.

EX XI·

(Yes, I shall die, but not by my desiring)

Seriousness naturally plays a greater part in the five-part madrigals, although the Roman public is never very far away from Marenzio's thoughts. Pictorialism and the mixed joys of pastoral love are still recurring motifs in the shaping of his style, and his skill in finding the appropriate musical image increases with his experience. Some of the images are conventional enough, but Marenzio tends to use them more consistently and with greater effect than other composers. The word 'eyes', for example, will nearly always gain its pair of semibreves. This was done by many others, but it is noticeable that in *Occhi lucenti e belli* he manages to integrate the 'eye-music' into the prolonged mood of serenity suggested by the verse.

EX XII

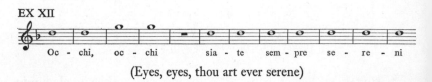

(Eyes, eyes, thou art ever serene)

Similarly in *Io piango*, the weeping eyes yet again are expressed by interlocked semibreves in the opening bars. Again Marenzio fully integrates the idea, with his initial chromatic change giving a chance of a wide range of harmony, especially when it is repeated with five voices instead of the initial four. And in this madrigal the word 'sigh', treated with its normal preceding rest, becomes a further extension of this beginning, for first it is repeated in a rising pattern, and then gains increased intensity with the very chromatic progression which opens the madrigal.

EX XIII

(and then she sighs)

Naturalistic symbols also abound, and some of these fit remarkably easily into the musical conception. The 'two fresh roses' in a Petrarch setting, *Due rose fresche e colte un paradiso*, give rise to a texture based on the twin motif which is a natural result of a five-voiced group with its two sopranos or tenors. The idea of dancing, which may appear whenever the verse conjures up a joyous emotion, finds equally appropriate expression in triple time. And whereas in the *Dolorosi martir* the change of motion is perhaps a little abrupt, Marenzio usually now develops the idea at great enough length to bring about a better sense of balance. The bagpipe sound suggested by a line in *O biondo Iddio* is typically extended over many bars of triple time, and so is the 'kissing' of the lovers in *Filli tu sei più bella*. Winds and waves always have some musical equivalent, the sea usually Mediterranean in its calm, consonant and even motion (rather like that in Wert's *Non è si denso velo* and Monteverdi's *Ecco mormorar l'onde*), the wind at times a little more animated, as in the sacred madrigal *Signor cui già fu poco*.

EX XIV

Height and depth are, of course, commonplace ideas. 'Scendi dal paradiso Venere' is a magnificent line for the musician to set and Marenzio finds a tremendous breadth in the measured descent of an octave imitated among all five voices. Occasionally the use of such clichés is not so happy, and virtuosity becomes a little empty. In another sacred madrigal, *E questo il legno*, it is not so much that the Saviour's sacrifice is seen in the very pastoral terms of the lamb going to be shorn, for Marenzio's setting seems to make Sannazaro's Arcadian idiom more dignified and suited to its subject. It is the mechanical application of octave leaps upwards and downwards for 'ciel' and 'terra', and the lack of their development, which seem to suggest too great an attention to detail and not enough concern for the overall emotional growth.

But such lapses are rare, and in the same madrigal Marenzio's marriage of the inner meaning of the words and the music can be seen in the fine climax. The verse speaks of the 'rare and new law' which Christ's sacrifice gave to mankind. The rarity and novelty of the chromatic scale are Marenzio's way of expressing this, and he repeats

13

his initial statement with a magical thickening of texture, which together with a modulation into a foreign key has a tremendous power.

EX XV

(O rare new law)

This shows a true appreciation of modern techniques, more assured than in *Dolorosi martir*, and the same can be said of the famous chromatic passage from another madrigal, *O voi che sospirate*. It is a setting of a verse from a long poem by Petrarch, the romantic's plea for death to release him from his misery. The optimist who dares to hope for the return of his love must

> . . . change for me his ancient song
> Since what makes others sad fills me with joy.

To change his ancient song can again only suggest chromaticism, since chromaticism has the association with the Renaissance experiments at the revival of Greek music. Marenzio indeed tries out what he conceives to be the Greek enharmonic genera, and if we can be sure that the result bears no resemblance to the music of the ancients, the passage is certainly enharmonic. It is one of the earliest examples to assume equal temperament, and its understanding of the results which can be obtained if G♯ is the same sound as A♭ shows a way to a new and successful technical power.

EX XVI

Such passages are all the more remarkable since Marenzio's idiom is by this time so firmly rooted in diatonicism—in our sense of the word. No doubt this came from the sheer singability of works written with harmonic simplicity, and able to use the modern resources of sequence and common cadential progressions. Marenzio's frankly popular style in the villanelle shows the extreme in this sort of writing. In these light, yet skilled, confections of madrigalian images the bass is liberated from its necessity to join in imitative counterpoint, and takes on its modern function. In *Amor è ritornato*, for example, only one imitative point is used in the bass, which for the rest acts as a harmonic unit. Its apparent resemblance to the upper parts comes from rhythmic similarities, which in turn are the result of setting the same words. But the smooth stepwise movement of the upper voices is lost as the bass is given leaps of fifths and fourths which give the effect of harmonic progressions on dominant, tonic and supertonic chords. In another number from the third book of villanelle, *Degli Occhi il dolce guido*, the canto fermo-like descending hexachord in the bass gives the opportunity for descending

EX XVII

(To depart or to fly)

15

sequences of the virile phrase in the soprano parts. This comes from the traditional movement in consecutive fifths of the older villanella, but the harmonic thinking in the passage is clearly Marenzian, and not in the least crude.

In more serious works sequences of this kind are worked in, sometimes to help in the extension of a phrase which requires weight, at other times to provide easy singing throughout the parts. In the sacred madrigal *Vergine Gloriosa* one passage is based on a descending figure which is so clearly chordal that it can be expressed in modern terms I–V–VI, III–IV, I–II. This progression would surely have been familiar to any continuo player in the eighteenth century, and here the function is to give a strong feeling of finality to the madrigal. In a secular madrigal from the second book for five voices the harmony has a vital part in the word-painting. *Io partirò* appears at first sight to be a conventional contrapuntal piece, with the bass joining in on equal terms with the other voices. A closer look reveals that only in the first phrase does the imitative tag manage to come also in the bass. For the rest, the imitations are never exact, and preserve the outlines of rhythm rather than the melodic shape. The reason is clear. Marenzio is thinking in terms of tonic and dominant chords, which when brought together cadentially are satisfying and when kept from this natural relationship are tense. A tonic pedal is appropriate for the relaxed phrase 'Love doth a work miraculous and blessed' (to use the translation of *Musica Transalpina*); a delay in the cadence, produced by continually hovering around the dominant without finally resolving it, adds to the frustrations of the dissonant setting of the 'But so great pains assail me'; and the insecurity of love is conveyed by the inconclusive ending on what seems to modern ears the dominant chord.[6]

It is this harmonic gift which makes possible the large-scale madrigals which are the glory of the young Marenzio. Such a tone picture as *Scaldava il sol* relies on the breadth of its harmonically conceived motifs much more than on counterpoint to conjure up the heat of some Mediterranean countryside at midday. The rays of the sun pour down with their scorching intensity through a descending sequential, solidly based phrase. The shepherd sings his villanella over a held drone and even the cricket's song is conceived in terms of a chord. With this material Marenzio can deploy a vast range of sonorities from the liveliness of the opening, with its pairs of voices gradually coming together at the first climax, through the full choir (with all the voices placed in their lowest registers) to paint the drowsy shepherd, and the single voice

[6] Modern reprint with English words edited by Alec Harman (London, 1953).

which reminds us that the silence is broken only by the insects. Conceived very strongly in terms of major tonality, every modulation and the occasional tinge of chromaticism becomes significant in maintaining the interest in the scene, pin-pointing, as it were, each object in this still landscape.

In the six-part madrigals this sense of harmony becomes even more important, since the larger resources require still more room for each motif to be developed, and for the contrasts of sonority, which are the main reason for writing in this medium, to achieve their effect. If the madrigals for five voices find their principal interest in expressing the detail of the verse, these larger works seem to explore form and tone quality more thoroughly. In some Marenzio repeats phrases so exactly that the architecture becomes the most important feature. In *Io morirò d'amore*,[7] for example, the verse contains little that can be painted in music, but its first line is repeated at the end, a hint which the composer follows. In another, *Piangea Filli*, Phyllis's cries to her beloved Thyrsis are repeated no less than four times, offering Marenzio a ready-made refrain effect. Several madrigals repeat the whole of their concluding phrases, interchanging the sopranos and tenors, or whichever parts are interlinked, in the manner of the canzonet. The scale on which these madrigals are built is, however, far from canzonet-like, and Marenzio's skill in finding new combinations of voices to build up a climax is supreme.

Nel più fiorito Aprile from the first book of madrigals for six voices is a fine example of the pastoral idiom adapted to this larger scale. The opening section is written only for four upper voices, which set the scene of the flowering meadows and sweetly singing birds of April in Italy. A cadence, then a change to triple time for 'singing their tuneful notes', bring in briefly the full ensemble, which again gives way to upper voices for an extended section. Gradually the lower voices join in the merrymaking, to reach a close on the dominant, and then the 'dolci amori' are celebrated with a splendid C major section, imitations flowing steadily as the short motif is worked through the voices. And since this motif is triadic, the bass is a solid anchor in its reiterations of the tonic. The net result is perhaps less subtle than a similar work for five voices, but in its extroversion this madrigal has the same enjoyable joie de vivre as we find in the English madrigalists when they, too, sing of springtime.

These high spirits permeate most of the six-part madrigals, even when Marenzio chooses love poetry which has a stronger feeling of

[7] ibid., 1954.

17

pathos and drama. In part this is due to his preoccupation with sonority rather than harmonies, and this comes naturally out of the medium. *Io morirò d'amore*, for example, is a poem which in a setting for five voices would probably have had its contrasts of the agony and solace in love expressed by contrasts between dissonance and consonance, and by variations of tempo. In this six-part setting 'death' provokes neither discord nor slow motion. The solace is found in a short melismatic phrase, but in general the contrasts are those of texture—either a straightforward change from upper voices to full ensemble, or a more intricate division of the voices into a variety of groups. Much the same can be said of *Qual vive Salamandra*, although here the 'burning of love' receives a more extended treatment, and the happiness which the lover feels in its flames merits an expansion in a tutti of a phrase sung earlier by the upper voices.

Just occasionally we see Marenzio exploring new potentialities. *Deh rinforzate* is a setting of a poem with a strong visual image, and as in the five-part books its potentialities are explored in full. A series of dissonant suspensions give power to the 'slow weeping' (largo pianto) of the poet; 'occhi' produces the inevitable pair of semibreves; 'the floods of tears' flow in downward scales. Then, towards the end, his pains consume him in cadential dissonances, which are simple yet very effective. From this we can be in no doubt that a more mature Marenzio will write such large-scale works within the power already present in these intimate surroundings.

EX XVIII

If such moments of intensity are rare, it is easy to see from the six-part madrigals why Marenzio became one of the most sought-after occasional composers of his time. There are at least half a dozen extant madrigals written to commemorate noble weddings, and in view of the mortality of this sort of music, surely more which never achieved print must have been sung at the banquets which were so often part of the celebrations. It was common in the sixteenth century for such works to be performed by large forces of singers and players, to make an overwhelming effect on an audience before which it was important to 'fare una bella figura'. Marenzio's wedding madrigals would have suited such large-scale performances admirably. Broad harmonic effects, no intricate counterpoint, and contrasts of texture are exactly what is needed, and if word painting can also be fitted in, this is a pleasing addition. *Scendi dal Paradiso* is a fine example of this manner. The opening theme paints Venus's descent from heaven in a steady and dignified figure; homophony, sometimes with the full chorus, at others with a voice missed out, dominates long sections, and always a slowly moving harmony allows for the spacious echo of a large banqueting hall. *Cedan l'antiche*,[8] written for a Roman wedding, has an even more splendid solemnity. The verse describes how yet one more triumphal procession is now a part of Roman history, and as the memories of past victories are invoked to add splendour to the present Marenzio slows his harmonies, so that for more than half a dozen bars a broad chord of C major provides the climax. The high notes of the sopranos were no doubt meant for doubling by cornetti and upper strings. Little imagination is needed to reconstruct the glory given by these instruments, together with trombones and chamber organs to mingle with the choir.

But for an Englishman the most famous of Marenzio's wedding madrigals will always be *Leggiadre ninfe e pastorelli*, written for the collection *Il Trionfo di Dori*, the model for *The Triumphs of Oriana*. The nymphs and shepherds dance and sing in praise of the bride, and there is the inevitable refrain 'Viva la bella Dori'. As in Weelkes's *As Vesta was from Latmos Hill descending*, there is a great deal of tone painting. 'The shady valley' where the scene is set provokes both black notation and downward leaps in all the voices, the 'crown' of flowers has a 'round' musical turn and the dancing is naturally done in triple time (complete with the hemiolia cadences fashionable for the 'alleluja' refrains in Venetian motets). Yet the differences from the Englishman become evident when the final rejoicing section arrives. Here is none of the contrapuntal dexterity of Weelkes, with his augmentations, stretti, and other devices. The Italian crowd merely shout their 'vivas' one after the other, relying on numbers and enthusiasm rather than skill. Marenzio is the modern master. Texture and sonority are his interests and counterpoint is now a minor resource.

By the time *Leggiadre ninfe* was first published in 1591 it was already something of an anachronism in Marenzio's work, for his style was changing rapidly, but in its combination of pictorialism and musicality

[8] Modern reprint edited by Lionel Benson in the Oriana Series (London, n.d.).

it sums up Marenzio's achievement in his early and middle years. It is an energetic, extravert piece, and this, too, is typical. Marenzio's music sometimes contains more pathos, but he is no tragedian. He is still a Roman in spirit, even though he is now an international figure. Indeed, it is his purity of style and his singability which made him so. For in England and Germany the modern Ferrarese musical dialect was too advanced and too dependent on an understanding of academic thought and the Italian language to have much effect. Anyone who was a musician could understand Marenzio's music. Nicholas Yonge knew Italian reasonably well—or at least the translator of *Musica Transalpina* did—and might possibly have chosen modern compositions with true comprehension of their welding together of verse and music. Thomas Watson, making his free translations for his *Italian madrigals Englished* in 1590, clearly misconceived completely the nature of this relationship, but this did not prevent him from picking some twenty of Marenzio's best madrigals for the anthology. Moreover, he was right. With wildly inaccurate translations—or perhaps played as viol music without any words at all—Marenzio's music can still stand by itself. This explains why Phalèse of Antwerp was eventually to reprint the nearly complete madrigal corpus of Marenzio, and why every anthologist from the mid-1580s sought one of his works, sometimes a new one, sometimes reprinting a madrigal from Marenzio's own collections.

It explains also why Marenzio's music affected other Roman composers. If his style had been too modern, an old man such as Palestrina would scarcely have bothered with him. As it was, in 1586 Palestrina's book of four-part madrigals shows that he had assimilated the principles of pictorialism and verbal expression, although the pastoral atmosphere did not attract him. *La cruda mia nemica* not only has an up-to-date emotional verse, but Palestrina sets the 'affective' words with dissonances, and achieves contrasts in the art of emotion. The word 'fuggir' (fly) in *I vaghi fiori* produces a suitable melisma, and 'lasso' (alas) a suspension. Other madrigalists writing for the anthology *Dolci affetti, madrigali a cinque voci de diversi eccellenti musici di Roma* (1586) show a lighter touch. Giovanni de Macque's *La mia leggiadra Clori*, for example, is in the diatonic pastoral idiom, complete with slow sections, interweaving sopranos, and a bass which often uses those leaps of fifths and fourths which give the feeling of a modern harmonic sense. Marenzio's style was now high fashion and there seems no reason why it should ever have changed.

II

IT is difficult to say when the delights of Arcady began to pall for Marenzio; impossible to say why. The easiest solution would be to accept Henry Peacham's romantic explanation:

. . . of stature and complexion he was a little and black man; he was organist in the Pope's chapel at Rome a good while; afterwards he went into Poland, being in displeasure with the Pope for overmuch familiarity with a kinswoman of his (whom the Queen of Poland sent for by Luca Marenzio afterward, she being one of the rarest women in Europe for her voice and lute). But returning, he found the affection of the Pope so estranged from him that hereupon he took a conceit and died. . . .[9]

Alas, Marenzio was, as far as the records show, never 'organist in the Pope's chapel', and his love for the prima donna may equally be legend rather than truth. Yet it is certain that a change took place in his music, and surely in his nature. After five most fecund years, suddenly there is a period of about two years when virtually nothing appeared from the presses. Then two books of madrigals came out and two minor volumes of villanelle. After this there was another silence of three years. He might have been composing steadily and not publishing his work, as Monteverdi did in the years between his third and fourth madrigal books, but then we might expect the backlog suddenly to pour from the houses of Gardano or Vincenti. In fact, very little fills Marenzio's last eight years. Less than a madrigal book a year appeared, something not uncommon for a slow composer like Monteverdi, but not in keeping with the normal habits of a productive composer such as Lassus or Marenzio. There is also a change in the contents of these volumes, which are very different in style from those early volumes which made him famous. The public felt this, too, for whereas, as we have seen, the earlier books went through large numbers of editions, and were known in England and Germany, the later madrigals were reprinted less often and never achieved such widespread fame.

It seems probable that Marenzio's new manner was in part influenced by a new atmosphere in Rome which began in the mid-1580s and continued until after his death. The Counter-Reformation, as a distinguished art historian has pointed out,[10] really began to affect artistic

[9] O. Strunk, *Source Readings in Music History* (New York, 1950), p. 335.
[10] R. Wittkower, *Art and Architecture in Italy 1600–1750* (London, 1958), p. 3.

thinking about this period, and there was an attempt at making both painting and architecture more intensely religious. In music, it is no coincidence that Marenzio produced his *Madrigali spirituali* within months of a similar set by Anerio. In the same year St. Philip Neri's Oratory had produced a book of spiritual songs, or Laudi, for domestic singing which had sold so well that it produced another shortly afterwards. Palestrina, whose early madrigals could hardly be called the most sensual of music, felt it necessary also in the same year (1584) to apologize for them in the preface of a book of motets.

There are too many poems with no other subject matter than loves alien to the Christian profession and name. These poems, written by men truly carried away by fury, corrupters of youth, have been chosen by a great many musicians as the material for their skill and industry, and while they have been distinguished by the praise of their talent, they have equally given offence to good and serious men. I blush and grieve to admit that I was once one of their number. But now, when past things cannot be changed and things cannot be undone, I have changed my ways. . . .[11]

That Marenzio had not changed *his* ways we have already seen from the extravagant pictorialism of his *Madrigali spirituali*; and yet even in this volume there are some signs of a new seriousness which may reflect Roman taste. In the second part of *E questo il legno* it is not so much the advanced chromaticisms setting 'O rara e nuova legge' or the dissonant 'a morte acerba e dura' which are remarkable. The purity of a later passage, 'Lassa mente infelice ogn'altra cura' (Leave, unhappy mind, all other cures), with its angelic sonority and fauxbourdon-like parallel harmonies, is the really uncommon feature of style.

EX XIX

Las - sa men - te in - fe - li - ce og-ni al - tra cu - ra,

Similarly the climax in *Signor cui già fu poco* is more restrained than we would expect from a master of pictorial harmony at this time.

EX XX

l'al - ma che plo - ra et gem - me ne le sue an-

[11] Strunk, op. cit., p. 323.

-go - scie e - stre - me

(the soul that weeps and laments in its extreme agonies)

So some change of style after the fallow period is not unexpected. More surprising is the fact that Marenzio was very conscious of the change, as the dedication of his next book of madrigals shows. It is significant that he chose the most knowledgeable of all musical noblemen, the Count Mario Bevilaqua of Verona, as the recipient of these madrigals 'lately composed by me in a manner rather different from those of the past, having, both by the imitation of the words and by the betterment of the style, given to them a (so to say) high seriousness'.

When a composer is conscious enough of a change to write of 'a manner rather different' we must immediately suspect that some revolution of mind or technique has taken place. This is not altogether true, for the madrigals are indeed only 'rather different'. There is no sudden experimental interest in chromaticism or dissonance, no discovery of new textures or sonorities. But there is a change of tone and mood, as can be seen at once in the verses he chooses. Admittedly they are rarely very far from the normal pastoral idiom. They speak of love and hope and despair in much the same way as do those of earlier madrigals. But they are more abstract and less concrete in their imagery, more concentrated in their emotional suggestions. *Interdette speranze*, to take a typical piece, is the setting of a quatrain from a Sannazaro sonnet with no pictorial possiblities at all. Its mood is serious and almost every word has its tense emotional connotation. 'Forbidden thought and vain desire', 'fallacious thoughts', 'sad tears', 'sorrowing sighs', these are the material for the composer. Another choice of Sannazaro's verse, *Fiere silvestre*, is a little more accommodating in its images of fields, steep roads and valleys; yet here again the words which set the emotional pattern are 'sad eyes' and 'lengthy weeping'.

If these poems are 'highly serious', Marenzio's treatment of them makes them more so. Whereas pictorialism had sometimes led to diffuseness in earlier works, he now strictly concentrates on the emotional power of these 'affective' words, each of which is given adequate musical treatment by which to create the mood. We have seen that in earlier madrigals Marenzio's tendency was to repeat the

23

pictorialisms at length, as in an aria, and to pass over the sadnesses rather quickly, almost as in a recitative. Here the reverse is true. In *Se la mia vita* the only concrete images are contained in the descriptive phrase 'the garlands, the green robes and the pallid face'. Marenzio paints them well enough: a wreathing motif for 'ghirlande' and chromaticism and white notes for the 'viso scolori'. But there is no repetition. All the ideas are dispatched quickly.

EX XXI

On the other hand, the lamentation which ends the piece is extended to double this length, as though the voices cannot bear the silence of their sadness.[12] And in this passage Marenzio's chromaticism has become less academic, more naturally integrated into his style. Instead of formal chromatic scales, the semitone is used to avoid the conventional cadence or harmony, to extend the phrase and to bring about a climax. He has not forgotten that the words 'mi fa' (it makes me) will suggest the solmization syllables to the singers. Each time they are set to E and F in an imitative phrase; but again this is not obvious as it is not pedantically pushed through all the parts.

It is this sense of proportion, and the sheer virtuosity of finding a phrase to fit the significant words without disturbing the musical flow, which are new in Marenzio's work. In *Per me dara tanta baldanza* the words 'tempo contrario' are expressed by a cross-rhythm which might in itself have a purely musical raison d'être. In *Fiere silvestre*[13] Marenzio completely ignores obvious picture-painting of 'acuti sassi' (steep rocks), and instead finds a motif which will give a semitone and declining scale to the 'dolorose rime' (sad verses) in the next line of the poem. 'Valley'

[12] Quoted by Einstein, *The Italian Madrigal*, ii, p. 665.
[13] Modern reprint in Einstein, *The Golden Age of the Madrigal* (New York, 1942).

24

does provoke an octave leap, but there is no extension of the idea, and the 'sighs' and 'weeping' of the succeeding phrase are given full rein in the chromatic and dissonant conclusion.

The other feature of this maturity lies in Marenzio's command of formal patterns. Sometimes, as in *Interdette speranze*, the form basically comes from the canzonet which, as Morley said, was by this time 'a counterfeit of the madrigal' and used madrigalian symbolism quite freely while preserving the extensive repetitions of succeeding phrases. But the first line of the verse is not repeated mechanically, being a development of a twin motif announced at the opening, and the restatement of the final section is given a surprising twist by four bars of coda, in which the slow-moving phrase acts as an augmentation summing up in a fugue. By these means the form is made more subtle. *Piango ch' Amor* has the seeds of musical form in the verse which uses the word 'sospiro' (sigh) in both its third and last lines. Most composers would have used the conventional 'sigh' motif, as indeed Marenzio did scores of times in his earlier madrigals. Few would have seen that the repetition of the word could suggest a satisfying musical shape, too. Marenzio makes sure that we notice the sigh, not only by giving it the customary preceding rest but also by a chromatic progression and an immediate restatement of the phrase. When he arrives at the final line of the poem he returns to the chromaticism, but by using a rhythm already involved in setting the penultimate phrase he introduces it naturally and without any formality, and it makes a remarkably satisfying conclusion to the madrigal.

This volume was clearly a turning-point in Marenzio's work, and if the change in the Roman cultural climate accounts for its increased seriousness, one feature is not explained completely. Why, after years of being its supreme master, did he suddenly turn his back on pictorialism? The answer is probably to be found in his contact with some Florentine musicians and amateurs who were discussing this very problem. We know that he was in touch with the Tuscan Court in the mid-1580s, because he dedicated an earlier book of five-part madrigals to the Grand Duchess Bianca Capello, and the year after he had completed this revolutionary book of *Madrigali a 4, 5, e 6 voci* he was engaged to compose much of the music for the usual celebrations on the occasion of the wedding of the new Grand Duke Ferdinand I to Christina of Lorraine, which eventually took place in 1589. Marenzio with several others composed the music for the intermezzi, which were produced in the most sumptuous manner, with an army of singers, players, scenic designers, and actors. This music, which survives in an unusually complete form, is on a huge, not to say grandiose, scale, with massive choruses for double choir and orchestral pieces for the vast ensemble assembled for the occasion.[14]

The earlier books of six-part madrigals have already shown us Marenzio's experience in composing this kind of music, and it is not surprising to find him given a lion's share in the commission. He provided the complete music for two intermezzi (more than anyone except the Florentine Malvezzi), consisting of seven madrigals, to one of which an introductory sinfonia is attached. Of these, four were massive pieces, composed for such large forces that the division into separated choirs 'alla Veneziana' was almost inevitable. The others were modestly scored, two of them being for small solo groups. The verse is, alas, only too occasional, and although by Rinuccini, later to become the librettist to Peri, Caccini, and Monteverdi, is sadly inferior to Marenzio's usual choice. Nor does the music measure up in any way to the subtle madrigalian art of his recent music. In *O figlio di Piero*, to take one of the larger pieces, the poet offers the opportunities for pictorialism in such words as 'heaven', 'earth', 'sweet sounds', all of which would have been treated at some length in earlier madrigals. Here they are merged into a general splendour of sound, which if undeniably effective is yet a little perfunctory. The cut-and-thrust between the three choirs which would have been exploited to the full by the Gabrielis is also neglected, as though Marenzio were not fully aware of its potentialities. The four-part texture of *O valoroso Dio* suits him better, and he uses the concertante interplay between the soprano voices very effectively in the manner of the Ferrarese composers. Again pictorialism is kept in the background, and the general tone is that of an accomplished writer of canzonets rather than of the profounder madrigalist of the recent volume for four, five and six voices.

This music, then, shows no signs of progress in his spiritual development, but technically Marenzio must have learned a great deal. Would he have had his work performed in Rome with (to quote a contemporary account) 'the exquisite graces and artifice of the two youths who are in the service of His Highness the Duke of Mantua'? The art of singing, and especially the art of singing elaborately ornamental lines, was surely more developed at the northern courts than anywhere else. Moreover, the participants in the production of these intermezzi were the members of the famed Camerata academy. Giovanni Bardi, Emilio de' Cavalieri, Peri, and Caccini had already embarked on the paths that were to lead

[14] All the music is reprinted, edited by D. P. Walker, in *Musique des Intermèdes de 'La Pellegrina'* (Paris, 1963).

to opera and monody, and even in the unlikely event of Marenzio not discussing the problems of the New Music with them, he had only to listen to some of the music they composed for this splendid occasion to realize that if the new philosophy put all his established principles in doubt it also had much to offer.

He may have met several of these composers earlier at home. The true teacher of the group, Girolamo Mei, was a courtier first of Cardinal Montepulciano and then of a wealthy nobleman, Giovanni Francesco Ridolfi, both of them living in Rome; and being an invalid, he spent his days being visited by Bardi, Strozzi, Galilei, and others, who discussed the music of the ancients with him. Mei was a true scholar and much more competent than earlier theorists to understand the peculiar nature of Greek music. From his studies it became clear to him and his circle that the precepts of Zarlino were no longer valid. If music was to be returned to its former glory described so eloquently by the Greek philosophers, the words which it was setting must acquire still more importance. They must be audible, and above all their emotional meaning and not merely their superficial images must be expressed. Galilei, writing in 1581 his *Dialogo . . . della musica antica, et della moderna*, was very scathing about the conventional innocence in tone painting:

They will say that they are imitating the words when among the conceptions of these there are any meaning 'to flee' or 'to fly'; these they will declaim with the greatest rapidity and the least grace imaginable. In connection with words meaning 'to disappear', 'to swoon', 'to die', or actually 'to be extinct' they have made the parts break off so abruptly, that instead of inducing the passion corresponding to any of these, they have aroused laughter and at other times contempt in the listeners, who felt that they were being ridiculed.[15]

This sort of thing was, of course, precisely what Marenzio had been doing, and even in his madrigal book for four, five, and six voices, with its increased awareness of the necessity to express the inner meaning of the verse, he nowhere approaches the Galileian principles. For Galilei wished at this time to abolish counterpoint completely, to substitute a declamatory style in which speech rhythms were the dominant feature and harmony was to take a secondary place. Marenzio would not agree to this, and yet he could not deny that there was much to be said for some change in attitude. So he preferred to compromise, and the madrigals of his post-Florentine period represent an attempt to try out the Camerata ideas while not abandoning conventional methods. In

[15] Strunk, op. cit., p. 316.

this he must have been encouraged by a knowledge that other northern composers, especially those of the courts of Mantua and Ferrara, were also interested in the problem and attempting new solutions which were not so extreme as Galilei's. The most influential of these was Giaches de Wert, an older man than Marenzio, whose early madrigals, dating back to the 1560s, were conventional enough before he, too, in the 1580s became interested in academic ideas. His experimental works, published in his eighth, ninth, and tenth madrigal books for five voices, attempt to make the words audible by crowding many syllables on to a single repeated note, and by making the texture simple and nearly homophonic.

EX XXII

He does not abolish counterpoint for purposes of contrast, and indeed, as in some of Marenzio's early music, his madrigals at times seem to embody an understanding of a recitative and aria relationship, the declamation giving vital words which must be heard and understood, the counterpoint providing a greater emotional power. In this he was followed by his most distinguished pupil, Monteverdi, whose crisis of style began during the period about 1590, exactly when Marenzio was evolving a new idiom.

Paradoxically, the most obvious sign that Marenzio was acquainted with the work of these composers is to be found in madrigals in which he does not try directly to emulate their ideas. These are a number of pieces which were written to be sung by the virtuoso ensemble of women at the court of the d'Este family at Ferrara. This ensemble consisted of three ladies who were celebrated throughout northern Italy for the dexterity of their voices, which could make the ornamental lines so beloved by the sixteenth-century audiences a sheer delight. Wert wrote a number of works for them, as did Luzzaschi (who provided keyboard accompaniment) and Monteverdi. Marenzio added to their repertoire some madrigals of great charm, which spring naturally in idiom from his earlier style. *Hor chi Clori beata* from his sixth book of five-part madrigals is one of the best of them, the sensuous quality of the three women's voices being exploited shamelessly for the delight of its sonority. Galilei would not have approved, but its strong diatonicism and regular rhythms and the balance of phrases achieved by melisma and verbal repetition make it one of the best of Marenzio's lighter madrigals.

EX XXIII

(Now fair Cloris curls her golden locks)

Là dove sono i pargoletti amori from the sixth book for six voices is in the same vein. The men are allowed slightly more interesting material (in *Hor chi Clori beata* they are relegated completely to the background), but again there is considerable interest in the bright sonorities of the upper voices. In this madrigal, indeed, pictorialism returns, although it never dominates; and musical imagery is not unexpected, for the verse is by Tasso, whose use of concrete images made him a favourite of many composers whose scruples were not disturbed by modern academicism.

Nevertheless, this modern academicism was gradually shaping Marenzio's new manner, and in many of the madrigals published after about 1592 we see the evidence that he was becoming an 'advanced' composer. One sign is that he now abandons the lighter poetry of Sannazaro in favour of the up-to-date Guarini, from whose *Pastor Fido* he chooses the laments and overwrought lyrics which were the stock in trade of all the madrigalists of the 1590s. This is significant, for Guarini is a poet of a very different kind from earlier pastoral lyricists. His work might almost be called 'mannerist'. From the simplicity of earlier pastoralism he distils an exaggerated emotional life. His shepherds and shepherdesses are often 'in extremis', the situations of his drama often melodramatic. Composers who set his work also tended to become melodramatic and mannerist, and until they discovered the even more

29

exaggerated emotional verse of Marini, found in his climaxes the starting-point for hitherto unsurpassed musical intensity.

Marenzio's settings of Guarini are not as 'modern' as those of Monteverdi or Pallavicino, nor as some of his own settings of other verse. Even so, the echoes of academic thought are clearly in his music. The most obvious of these concerns texture. Counterpoint has now been reduced to harmony—that is, it is no longer the interplay between voices that determines the strength of the music so much as the relationship between a melodic upper part and a harmonic ebb and flow dominated by the bass. In *Deh, Tirsi anima mia* from the sixth book for five voices some two-thirds of the madrigal is written homophonically, with identical rhythms in all the parts. There is an occasional change of sonority, as the bass or tenor is left out, to lighten the texture. Occasionally a part will anticipate the upper voice by a syllable, or vice versa. Nevertheless, the effect is one of quasi-monody, in which the audibility of the words is of paramount importance. There is only one melisma in the soprano part in some fifty bars, but there are a number of elisions, so that the effect of speech rhythm is never far away. The method of melodic organization has also been adapted to these new methods. Phrases are clear-cut, often falling into 4- and 8-bar patterns. When a phrase demands development it is repeated, enhanced by a change of pitch in a way impossible in truly contrapuntal music, but normal in any harmonically conceived style.

EX XXIV.

Deh, qual vendett' ha - ver puoi tu mag - gio - re,   Deh, qual vendett' ha -

-ver puoi tu mag - gio - re.

(Alas, what greater revenge could you have)

The concern for melodic expression is to be found in another Guarini lament, *Cruda Amarilli*, published in 1595 in the seventh book of madrigals for five voices. In this Marenzio is not so strict with himself, and there is more melodic movement in inner voices. But the restraint by which he avoids pictorialism is very much in contrast with his earlier style. The verse contains the 'white lilies', 'the crying of beaches and mountains', 'the murmuring of the winds', in other words, practically the whole apparatus of verbal suggestion which had formerly so attracted him. He now rejects them all. The lilies merit no 'eye-music'; the mountains do rise, but by no notable leaps; and the murmuring of the winds passes by in the general recitative. The emotional outpourings of the bereaved lover gain more attention. His cry 'ahi, lasso' is dissonant, and when the fountains weep in sympathy with him the motion is slow, and turns to the subdominant (one can now truthfully call it this). It is the general unity of mood which conveys the strength of emotion, rather than the details of word-painting. In another way too the madrigal is quite unusual. Except at a climax, it is (like *Deh, Tirsi*) almost entirely consonant. The continuous agonies of the Mantuan settings by Monteverdi and Pallavicino are conspicuously absent. A comparison of the latter's climax, its continuous semitonal dissonance, minor key, and downward leap of a seventh in the bass, with the simplicity of Marenzio's steady and major-key movement shows us the classical standpoint of the Roman composer still in command.

EX XXV
(a)

di - ran - no i   miei   la - men - - - ti

(b)

di - ran - no i   miei   la - men - - ti.

(They will speak of my lamenting)

Again it is the melody, and principally the soprano melody, which is the important means of expression. The occasional chromaticism, the downward leap of the sixth, the breaking off before an 'affective' word such as 'lamento', the changes in movement, are the real stuff of the madrigal, which could easily be performed by a solo voice and four accompanying viols without damage to its meaning.

The effect of this concentration on melody is curious. If we compare these madrigals with, say, *Dolorosi martir*, the poem of which offered much the same opportunities to the composer, Marenzio seems now oddly chaste. The early work has an erotic, physical agony, while the later madrigals are resigned in sorrow, and when he turns away from Guarini, we notice the development of this abstraction. Marenzio now becomes obsessed (if that is not too strong a term) with increasing age and with death. This 'death' is no erotic symbol in disguise, but clearly the end of life itself as we can see from the choice of Petrarch's sestina, *Giovane Donna*, as the poem for the centre piece of the sixth book of madrigals for six voices. In this the poet ponders over the effect his beloved has had on him in the seven years he has known her, and how, even though he has not seen her, the agony in his heart has continued to feed on her remembered image. He thinks about the transcience of man and on his old age when his locks will be white, and only memory will sustain 'the fire within'.

> But since time is flying and the years depart
> Yes, to death each one must come,
> Be they bearers of brown or white locks.

The emphasis on 'white' images, the constant references to snow and ice take away any suggestion of sensuousness. If this is a love lyric, it is one which is as far from Marenzio's earlier choice as it could possibly be.

Marenzio's setting is equally far away from his early music. His style is austere to the point of being enigmatic. He plans the work as a series of seven madrigals, interdependent in their changes of tonality and in the long-range emotional construction of the whole. This makes it one of the longest works of its time, the only comparable series being music with serious religious connotations, such as the Lassus settings of the Penitential Psalms, or the various settings of Petrarch's *Vergine bella*, a favourite Counter-Reformation text after Rore had set the fashion in the 1550s. Marenzio seems to draw together all the techniques which he had been studying in the last fifteen years. His opening madrigal, in which the meeting with the beloved, then young and fair, is remembered, is contrapuntal, with an academic flavour in the way that one part moves slowly while another provides the decorations (almost as a beginner learned the improvisatory techniques so much a part of sixteenth-century musical practice). The emotional level is deliberately kept low, as though it is to prove an introduction to the second madrigal, which matches the snowy images of the verse with slow (white) notes. This is a mainly homophonic piece, and the way the emotion is heightened through harmonic means reminds us of the recent 'camerata' period of the composer.

(. . . until we see the fire freeze, the snow burn)

The third section again returns to an earlier style, frankly painting the images—a violent shift to triple time and black notation for the words '. . . death comes to the dark ones', a return to normality and white notes for the '. . . and to the white haired', and a series of close canons for the word 'seguirò' (I shall follow). Such comparative happiness lasts but a short time. By the end of the section gloom has returned, and is intensified in the fourth madrigal, which has a very dissonant climax. Calm is now completely gone. The opening of the fifth section wrenches the tonal centre from G to E with an abrupt chromatic change, and as the image of the beloved as she was seven years ago torments him, both dissonance and a broken-up melody for his sighs turn the knife in the wound. The madrigal ends inconclusively, as though the agony is too great for a return immediately to the relaxation of the perfect cadence. The sixth section is one of the most extended of all madrigals, its climax setting the words 'sempre piangendo andrò' (I shall go always weeping) over some twenty bars of slow movement, and deriving its power from the sheer musical ability to add new counterpoints to the basic contrapuntal tag, and to frustrate the cadence with a dissonance or chromatic change. In the final section more conventionally diatonic tags are developed contrapuntally and academically to bring the cycle to rest. Significantly, because Marenzio adheres to no specific theories covering the relationship of words and music, the work shows a huge variety of textures. As a concrete image can at times bring home a philosophic point in otherwise abstract verse, so can eye-music and pictorialism, when they do not dominate the comprehensive musical pattern as they did sometimes in Marenzio's earlier music, emerge as a way of quickly establishing an emotional point. The homophony of the 'academic' madrigal is put to good use as a means of putting less emphasis on words than the expansion which imitative counterpoint suggests. Thus the *Giovane Donna* is one of Marenzio's balanced master-pieces, and one of the most impressive monuments of the genre.

It was by no means the end of Marenzio's development. In the same book of six-part madrigals another cycle explores new paths. *Se quel dolor* is a sequence in ten sections of a 'capitolo' of Girolamo Trojano. The theme here is even more strongly that of the advance towards death. 'Pain is at our birth and in our living', and while in *Giovane Donna* the despair is no deeper than nostalgia, in this cycle it is more profound. To express this, Marenzio for the first time takes to the tech-nique of mannerism as developed by the Mantuans. In this the indi-vidual vocal line is often fragmentary and lacking in continuous movement, for it is the total effect which is important. The singer is no longer the important patron whose convenience is the primary con-sideration, and while the angularities of Wert and Pallavicino are severer than Marenzio ever uses, his lines are often made awkward by chromatic movement and unstable tonality. The harmony has become equally full of asperities, and is similar to that found in the madrigals which Monteverdi was writing about this time. The pin-pricks to which Artusi so objected in the latter's *Cruda Amarilli* and *Era l'anima mia* are nothing like as severe as the following passage from *Se quel dolor*.

EX XXVII

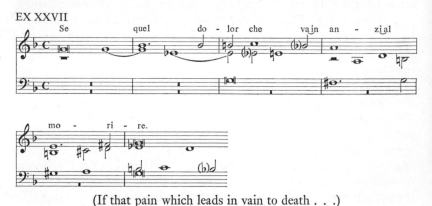

(If that pain which leads in vain to death . . .)

Admittedly, there is scarcely a progression which cannot in itself be defended by rules acknowledged by the conventional theorists (although the taking of a dissonance on the up-beat and then making it a normal suspension is not exactly usual even at this time). Yet the extended nature of the passage and the way the expectation of the dissonance is consistently denied make this comparable with anything the moderns were writing in the 1590s, with about half of the chords textbook dissonances. The use of diminished intervals which give the effect of chords of the seventh is common enough to make anyone wonder why Monteverdi's 'discovery' of the dominant seventh is so celebrated.

EX XXVIII

(And when [the thread] of life is cut)

As in the madrigals of the 1587 era, one feels that these mannerist madrigals, published after another break, are the result of another conscious change of attitude on Marenzio's part; and again it may well be that the Camerata theorists were responsible. Galilei, just before his death in 1591, had intended to publish a treatise on counterpoint. As we might expect, it is not orthodox in its teaching, and although, as one scholar has noted,[16] the title mentions 'counterpoint', it is, in fact, one of the earliest (if not the very earliest) harmony books to be written, and its main purpose was to revise the rules concerning dissonance. Galilei has no doubt that a free treatment is not only possible but desirable:

Whenever two or more notes move over one another gracefully according to the decorum of the art of counterpoint, whatever dissonance occurs among them not only will be tolerated by the sense, but it will take delight in it. All extremes, however, should be avoided with mature judgement as vicious. . . .

In defining the possibilities, he sees no reason why diminished intervals should not take their places among ordinary dissonances, and, provided

[16] C. Palisca, 'Vincenzo Galilei's Counterpoint Treatise: a code for the *Seconda Pratica*', *Journal of the American Musicological Society* ix (1956), p. 81.

they are resolved correctly may even be considered consonant. Double and triple suspensions are allowed and sevenths are now to be integral parts of certain chords. It is possible for a severe dissonance to be resolved by a leap to any consonant note of the next chord. In other words, all the careful gradualness in harmony advocated by Zarlino and the conservative theorists could be completely disregarded.

Monteverdi was the composer who most readily took to those ideas. Marenzio, some twelve years older, found it harder to absorb them fully, but there are some passages in his advanced madrigals which are so close to Galilei's precepts that it can have been no coincidence. One progression in *I temo di cangiar* is identical with one of Galilei's examples;[17] another of these produces exactly the same asperity as we have seen in the passage quoted from *Se quel dolor*;[18] and if Marenzio would not take the final stage of irregular resolution of dissonance in his 1594 book this was soon to come.

It came in the final volume of his madrigals to be published in his lifetime, his ninth book of madrigals for five voices. It is a remarkable collection in many ways, full of the gloom which had increasingly affected his music. Dedicated appropriately to Vincenzo Gonzaga, it is his most Mantuan set, the one nearest in style to Pallavicino, Wert, and Monteverdi. The verse is very much the kind these composers were setting, the poems full of the 'affective' words which allowed the musicians to show their virtuosity. Even the more relaxed verses, such as Guarini's *Credete voi ch'i'vivo*, contain potentialities for the advanced style. In this madrigal not only is there the usual 'dying' and 'death' image for Marenzio to display his new freedom of dissonance. When he thinks of the beloved it is in itself enough to stimulate a very strange harmonic progression, with a 'forbidden' leap in the soprano and tenor and a bitter-sweet false relation between soprano and alto.

EX XXIX

a - nima ca - ra in vo - i

The showpiece of the volume is the setting of Petrarch's *Solo e pensoso*, a sonnet which once would have offered Marenzio ample

[17] v. Palisca, Ex. 8b.   [18] ibid., Ex. 20c.

opportunities for painting its images of 'mountain, wood, valley and flood', the slow tread of the lover and the 'wild and savage paths' which are his consolation. But now it is the abstraction of his flight from 'the world's prying eye' and the loneliness of the deserted fields which are the musician's material. The loneliness is felt in the single rising chromatic scale in the soprano, which none of the other parts dare to follow, the slow steps of the lover in its measured chromatic descent.

EX XXX

(I go measuring my slow and reluctant steps)

In the second part word-painting finds its place. The 'mountains' stimulate an upward leap, the 'rivers' find a natural expression in a melismatic run; but Marenzio's purpose is plainly to contrast these images of happiness with the 'wild and savage paths' of the harmonic movement in the slow-moving passage to follow. And the final stroke of genius is the prolonged imitative conclusion, which by the very extensiveness of the musical development seems the proper setting of the final lines of the verse, in which the lover can find no way to forget his pain:

> A way so rough that there love cannot go
> Communing with me the long day and night.

Here Marenzio's perennial interest in musical device finds its reward. Wert had done a setting of this poem which is extravagantly mannerist in its treatment of the words, even to the point of ending with a solo voice to express the loneliness of the poet. Magnificent though this is, Marenzio's is more satisfying. The wild leaps and strange modulations of Wert seem today a trifle freakish, as though they must remain an

37

academic document tailored for their original audience of noble intellectuals. Marenzio requires no narrow audience; his musicality in itself is enough to explain his profoundly felt meaning to the least intellectual singer and listener.

Only in one number in the final book does he overstep these bounds and become himself a mannerist. It is a setting of a verse which perhaps may have been the first to inspire a madrigal of the 'seconda prattica'. Petrarch's *Crudele acerbo, inexorabil morte* had been set by de Rore in the 1550s. With its opening leaps of a sixth, its frankly colourist approach to the words, this madrigal had been a landmark which was acknowledged by all the later 'advanced' composers and theorists. Monteverdi, defending himself from the attacks of the conservative Artusi, was proud to claim that he was the latest in a line of moderns which went back to de Rore, and this madrigal was one which must have had so much to do in revealing a new path. The verse from Petrarch's sestina so closely fits in with the mood of those chosen by Marenzio in the 1590s that it is no surprise that he also attempted a setting.

> O cruel, grim, inexorable Death
> How hast thou dried my every source of joy
> And left me to drag on a life of tears. . . .

Nor is it a surprise that Marenzio begins with the sixth leaps of de Rore, for famous madrigals of this kind were often made into a 'parody' (in the sixteenth-century sense of the word). This parodistic element soon disappears. The 'dark days and nights of sadness' provoke an extremism scarcely equalled even by the Mantuan or Ferrarese composers. Gone is contrapuntal logic, the chromaticisms seem almost haphazard, leading to cadences in strange keys; difficult melodic leaps are commonplace; the melody breaks off in mid-cadence, as though a sense of completion no longer matters. The climax conveys a lack of direction which is terrifying.

EX XXXI

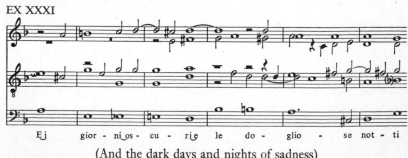

Ej   gior - ni_os - cu - ri̯e le do - glio - se not - ti

(And the dark days and nights of sadness)

Sometimes a drastic change of style seems to be the result of musical discoveries or experiments. Monteverdi's third book and Gesualdo's third and fourth books of madrigals might possibly be considered such speculative works. This 'opus ultimum' of Marenzio, however, is so mature, and contains so much that is obviously technically assured, that we must assume his innovations to be due to some spiritual crisis. Perhaps this wild madrigalian contemplation of inexorable death was premonitory. The madrigal book was dedicated to the Mantuan Prince on 11 May 1599. Within four months the composer was dead. But to prevent us thus sentimentalizing this last published work, a letter of a minor Venetian poet, Angelo Grillo, tells of more madrigals, which have now disappeared:

The other day the last works of Luca Marenzio of honoured memory came to me by chance—madrigals which were almost all composed to poems of mine. Admittedly it was juvenile poetry set to mature music, for they were written at a time when not only the poetry but also the poet was immature. So much the more then do I stand in his debt to that immortal swan, who chose to intone his deathsong, so to speak, to the verses of a cricket (grillo), verses which he made sweet and immortal through his melody. Such men should not die. . . .[19]

That Marenzio should set Grillo's verse to music makes us wonder in which way he would have developed, for Grillo was later a friend of Strozzi and Rinuccini, and Caccini also set some of his poems to music. Indeed, the only setting of Grillo by Marenzio that we know is a sweetly simple madrigal (or canzonet, to give a better title) in his eighth book for five voices, which if notated in the modern manner of the post-1600 composers looks very like the arias of *Le Nuove Musiche*.[20]

EX XXXII

(Know not which are the roses and which is you)

Marenzio was, then, a developing composer. Whether, in fact, he would have taken the final steps to write the more extreme New Music is another matter. He was far from the dilettantism that was the basis of

[19] A. Einstein, *Essays on Music*, English edition (London, 1958), p. 171.
[20] The original is reprinted in Marenzio, *Madrigali a cinque e a sei voci*, ed. Mompellio (Milan, 1953), p. 6.

Florentine thinking, and looking at his career as a whole, it appears that he was more of the pure musician than Monteverdi, in whose mind academic speculation played a large part until the end. Marenzio was indeed acknowledged as a modern in the famous preface to Monteverdi's first book of *Scherzi Musicali*; but Banchieri, writing about the same time, prefers to place him by the side of Palestrina as a classic. This is perhaps nearer the truth. For his real fame still came from his earlier music. When the collectors of those anthologies with the delightfully poetic names of *Nervi d'Orfeo* or (for the German public) *Lieblicher, Welscher Madrigalien auss den berühmtester Musicis Italicis* chose his music, it was to the singable works of the 1580s that they turned. When the editors of the volumes of religious 'contrafactur' wished to give to the public favourite madrigals to sing to their respectably devotional verses, it was in *Leggiadre Ninfe*, *Dolorosi martir* and the other works of this style that they found their material. When Francis Tregian junior was whiling away the weary years in the Fleet Prison by copying his immense virginal book, he found that Giles Farnaby had produced some happy arrangements of the *Tirsi* madrigals which were well worth his trouble; and he also took care to add no less than fifty of Marenzio's villanelle and the whole of his book of four-part madrigals to the collection of vocal music which he was putting into score.

For this reason perhaps Marenzio is still underrated. The famous names of his time are either the revolutionaries and advanced composers, or those composers whose work has been preserved and cherished by the traditions of church music. The fact that Marenzio was the first secular composer has probably led us astray, for we expect more drama from such music if it is to stand comparison with later music of a humanistic kind. It is symptomatic that we can now buy the complete works of Monteverdi and Palestrina, and that Stravinsky's occasional investigations of the past have led him to Gesualdo. Only the earlier works of Marenzio are at present available (in an impractical edition made over thirty years ago) for the student to see in score. Yet what Henry Peacham called his 'delicious air and sweet invention' are only one side of Marenzio's work; and we shall realize his full greatness only when we discover in his later music that he was also a very human being.

LIST OF WORKS

1577 One madrigal in *Il primo fiore della Ghirlanda Musicale*, Venice, herede di Scotto.

1580 *Il 1° libro de Madrigali a 5 voci*, Venice, Gardano.

1581 *Il 2° libro de Madrigali a 5 voci*, Venice, Gardano.
Il 1° libro de Madrigali a 6 voci, Venice, Gardano.

1582 *Il 3° libro de Madrigali a 5 voci*, Venice, Gardano.
Reprint of *Il 1° libro de Madrigali a 5 voci*, Venice, Gardano.
Two madrigals in *Il Lauro Secco*, Ferrara, Baldini.
Two madrigals in *Dolci Affetti Madrigali a cinque voci*, Venice, herede di Scotto.
One madrigal arranged for lute in *Novae tabulae musicae*, Strasbourg, Jobin.

1583 Reprint of *Il 2° libro de Madrigali a 5 voci*, Venice, Gardano.
Four madrigals in *Harmonia Celeste di diversi eccellentissimi musici*, Antwerp, Phalèse and Bellère.
One madrigal in *Il Lauro Verde*, Ferrara, Baldini.
One madrigal in *De Floridi Virtuosi d'Italia*, Venice, Vincenti and Amadino.
One madrigal in *Li Amorosi Ardori di Diversi Eccellentissimi Musici*, Venice, Gardano.
One madrigal in *Musica divina di XIX autori illustri*, Antwerp, Phalèse and Bellère.

1584 *Il 4° libro de Madrigali a 5*, Venice, Vincenti and Amadino.
Reprint of *Il 1° libro de Madrigali a 6*, Venice, Gardano.
Il 2° libro de Madrigali a 6, Venice, Gardano.
Madrigali spirituali . . . a 5, Rome, Gardano.
Il 1° libro delle Villanelle a 3, raccolte de Ferrante Franchi, Venice, Vincenti and Amadino.
Two madrigals in *Spoglia Amorosa*, Venice, erede di Scotto.
Four madrigals arranged for lute in *Il 1° libro de intavolatura da liuto*, Venice, erede di Scotto.

1585 *Il 2° libro delle Canzonette alla Napoletana a 3*, Vincenti and Amadino.
Il 3° libro delle Villanelle a 3, Rome, Gardano.
Reprint of *Il 1° libro delle Villanelle a 3*, Venice, Vincenti.
Four madrigals in *Symphonia Angelica*, Antwerp, Phalèse and Bellère.
Two madrigals in *Spoglia Amorosa Madrigali a cinque*, Venice, herede di Scotto.
Two madrigals in *Canzonette Spirituali de Diversi, a tre voci, libro primo*, Rome, Gardano.
Motectorum pro festis totius anni, Venice, Gardano and Amadino.
One madrigal in Moscaglia, *Il secondo libro de Madrigali a quattro voc* Venice, Vincenti and Amadino.

1586 Reprint of *Il 1° libro de Madrigali a 5*, Venice, Vincenti and Amadino.
Reprint of *Il 1° libro delle Villanelle a 3*, Venice, Vincenti.
One madrigal in *Corona di dodici sonetti di Gio. Battista Zuccarini*, Venice, Gardano.
One madrigal in *I Lieti Amanti*, Venice, Vincenti and Amadino.
One madrigal in *Musica spirituale*, Venice, Gardano.

41

Two madrigals in *Diletto Spirituale*, Rome, van Buyten.
Two madrigals in *Diletto Spirituale* . . . *con l'intavolatura del cimbalo et liuto*, Rome, Verovio.
One madrigal in *De Floridi Virtuosi d'Italia, il primo libro de Madrigali a cinque voci*, Venice, Vincenti and Amadino.

1587   *Il 4º libro delle Villanelle a 3*, Venice, Vincenti.
Il 5º libro delle Villanelle a 3, Venice, L'Heredi di Scotto.
Reprint of *Il 1º libro de Madrigali a 5*, Venice, Vincenti and Amadino.
Reprint of *Il 2º libro de Madrigali a 5*, Venice, Vincenti.
Reprint of *Il 2º libro delle Canzonette alla Napoletana a 3*, Venice, Vincenti.
Reprint of *Il 3º libro delle Villanelle a 3*, Rome, Vincenti.
Four madrigals in *Primus liber suavissimus praestantissimorum*, Erfurt, Baumann.
Il 4º libro de Madrigali a 6, Venice, Vincenti.
Reprint of *Il 4º libro de Madrigali a 6*, Venice, Amadino.
Reprint of *Motectorum pro festis* . . ., Venice, Amadino.

1588   *Madrigali a 4, 5, e 6, lib. 1*, Venice, Vincenti.
Reprint of *Il 1º libro de Madrigali a 5 voci*, Venice, Vincenti.
Reprint of *Madrigali Spirituali* . . . *a 5*, Venice, Scotto.
Reprint of *Il 1º libro della Villanelle a 3*, Venice, Vincenti and Amadino.
Il 5º libro de Madrigali a 5, Venice, L'Heredi di Scotto.
Seven madrigals in *Musica Transalpina*, London, East.
Thirteen madrigals in *Gemma Musicalis*, Nürnberg, Gerlach.
One madrigal in *L'Amorosa Eto rappresentata da' più celebri musici d'Italia*, V. Sabbio, Brescia.
Three motets in *Continuatio cantionum sacrarum*, Nürnberg, Gerlach.

1589   Sixteen madrigals in *Liber secundus Gemmae Musicalis*, Nürnberg, Gerlach.
One madrigal in *Musicale Essercitio di Ludovico Balbi*, Venice, Gardano.
One madrigal in *Le Gioie Madrigali a cinque voci*, Venice, Amadino.
One madrigal in *Ghirlanda di Fioretti Musicali*, Rome, Verovio.
Reprint of *Il 4º libro de Madrigali a 5*, Venice, Vincenti and Amadino.
Reprint of *Il 1º libro de Villanelle a 3*, Venice, Vincenti and Amadino.

1590   Two madrigals in *Dialoghi Musicali*, Venice, Gardano.
Five madrigals in *Symphonia Angelica*, Antwerp, Phalèse and Bellère.
Twenty madrigals in *The first sett of Italian Madrigalls Englished*, London, East.
One madrigal in *Selva di varia ricreatione di Horatio Vecchi*, Venice, Gardano.

1591   *Il 5º libro de Madrigali a 6*, Venice, Gardano.
Eight pieces in *Intermedii et concerti*, Venice, Vincenti.
Reprint of *Il 3º libro de Madrigali a 5*, Venice, Vincenti.
Reprint of *Il 5º libro delle Villanelle a 3*, Venice, Gardano as *Villanelle et Arie*.
Five madrigals in *Melodia Olympica*, Antwerp, Phalèse and Bellère.
One madrigal in *La Ruzina*, Venice, Gardano.
One madrigal in *Canzonette a quattro voci*, Rome, Verovio.
One madrigal in *Canzonette per cantar et sonar di liuto, libro terzo*, Venice, Vincenti.
One madrigal in *Il Lauro Verde*, Antwerp, Phalèse and Bellère.
One madrigal in *Canzonette Spirituali a 3*, Rome, Verovio.

1592   Reprint of *Il 2º libro delle Canzonette alla Napoletana a 3*, Venice, Vincenti.
Reprint of *Il 3º libro delle Villanelle a 3*, Rome, Gardano.
Reprint of *Il 4º libro delle Villanelle a 3*, Venice, Vincenti.
Reprint of *Motectorum pro festis totius anni*, Venice, Amadino.
Motectorum lib. secundus (lost).

One madrigal in *La Gloria Musicale*, Venice, Amadino.
One madrigal in *Il Devoto Pianto della Gloriosa Vergine*, Rome, Verovio.
One madrigal in *Spoglia Amorosa a 5*, Venice, Gardano.
One motet in Conforti, *Psalmi, Motecta, Magnificat et antiphona*, Rome, Coattino.
One madrigal in *Il Trionfo di Dori*, Venice, Gardano.
Six pieces in *Novum pratum musicum*, Antwerp, Phalèse and Bellère.

1593 Reprint of *Il 2º libro de Madrigali a 5*, Venice, Gardano.
Reprint of *Il 4º libro de Madrigali a 6*, Venice, Gardano.
Eight madrigals in *Harmonia Celeste*, Antwerp, Phalèse and Bellère.
One madrigal in *Florindo e Armilla*, Venice, Amadino.
Two madrigals in *Nuova Spoglia Amorosa*, Venice, Vincenti.
Il 1, 2, 3, 4 e 5 lib. de Madrigali a 5, ridotti in un corpo, Antwerp, Phalèse.
One madrigal arranged for lute in Terzi, *Intavolatura di liutto*, Venice, Amadino.

1594 *Il 6º libro de Madrigali a 5*, Venice, Gardano.
Reprint of *Il 4º libro de Madrigali a 5*, Venice, Gardano.
Reprint of *Il 5º libro de Madrigali a 5*, Venice, Gardano.
Collected edition of *Madrigali a sei voci in un corpo ridotti*, Antwerp, Phalèse and Bellère.
Three madrigals in *Florilegium omnis fere generis cantionum*, Cologne, Greuenbruch.

1595 *Il 7º libro de Madrigali a 5*, Venice, Gardano.
Il 6º libro de Madrigali a 6, Venice, Gardano.
Reprint of *Il 3º libro de Madrigali a 5*, Venice, Gardano.
Reprint of *Il 1º libro delle Villanelle a 3*, Venice, Vincenti.
Two reprints of *Il 5º libro de Madrigali a 6*, Venice, Gardano and Scotto.
Completorium et Antiphonae 6v. (lost).

1596 Reprint of *Il 1º libro de Madrigali a 6*, Venice, Scotto.
Reprint of *Il 2º libro de Madrigali a 6*, Venice, Scotto.
Reprint of *Il 4º libro delle Villanelle a 3*, Venice, Gardano.
One madrigal in *Madrigali a otto voci*, Antwerp, Phalèse.
Three madrigals in *Paradiso Musicale*, Antwerp, Phalèse.
One madrigal in *Vittoria Amorosa*, Venice, Vincenti.

1597 Reprint of *Il 2º libro delle Canzonette alla Napoletana a 3*, Venice, Vincenti.
Reprint of *Il 3º libro delle Villanelle a 3*, Rome, Gardano.
Five madrigals in *Fiori del Giardino*, Nürnberg, Kauffmann.
Three madrigals in *Musica Transalpina, The Second Book*, London, East.
Two madrigals in *Il Vago Alboreto*, Antwerp, Phalèse.
One madrigal in *Canzonette a quattro voci*, Venice, Vincenti.

1598 *Il 8º libro de Madrigali a 5*, Venice, Gardano.
One madrigal in Morley, *Madrigals to five voyces*, London, East.
Two motets in *Sacrae symphoniae, diversorum excellentissimorum authorum*, Nürnberg, Kauffmann.

1599 *Il 9º libro de Madrigali a 5*, Venice, Gardano.
One piece in *Tempio Armonico*, Rome, Mutii.
One motet in *Motetti et salmi a otto voci*, Venice, Vincenti.
Two madrigals in Bargnani, *Canzonette, Arie et Madrigali*, Venice, Amadino.
Three madrigals arranged for lute in Terzi, *Il secondo libro de intavolatura*, Venice, Vincenti.

1600 One piece in *Magnificat octo tonorum*, Nürnberg, Kauffmann.
Reprint of *Il 1º libro de Madrigali a 5*, Venice, Scotto.
Reprint of *Il 2º libro de Madrigali a 6*, Venice, Gardano.

43

Reprint of *Il 1° libro delle Villanelle a 3*, Venice, Gardano.
Reprint of *Il 2° libro delle Canzonette alla Napoletana a 3*, Venice, Gardano.
Reprint of *Il 3° libro delle Villanelle a 3*, Rome, Gardano.
Reprint of *Il 4° libro delle Villanelle a 3*, Venice, Gardano.
Reprint of *Il 5° libro delle Villanelle a 3*, as *Villanelle et Arie*, Venice, Gardano.
Reprint of *Il 7° libro de Madrigali a 5*, Venice, Gardano.
Two motets in *Sacrarum symphoniarum continuatio*, Nürnberg, Kauffmann.
Seven madrigals in *Flores musicae*, Heidelberg, Vögelin.
Two madrigals in *Florum musicae*, Heidelberg, Vögelin.
One madrigal in *De Floridi Virtuosi d'Italia*, Antwerp, Phalèse.

1601 Reprint of *Il 9° libro de Madrigali a 5*, Venice, Gardano.
One madrigal in *Ghirlanda di madrigali a sei voci*, Antwerp, Phalèse.
Collected edition of *Madrigalia quinque vocum*, Nürnberg, Kauffmann.
Nine madrigals in *Florida, sive cantiones* . . ., Utrecht, Roy and Rhenen.

1602 Reprint of *Il 1° libro de Madrigali a 5*, Venice, Gardano.
One piece in *Opus melicum, methodicum et plane novum*, Magdeburg, Seydner.

1603 Reprint of *Il 2° libro de Madrigali a 5*, Venice, Raveri.
Reprint of *Il 1° libro de Madrigali a 6*, Venice, Gardano.
Reprint of *Il 4° libro de Madrigali a 6*, Venice, Scotto.
Reprint of *Il 6° libro de Madrigali a 5*, Venice, Gardano.
Reprint of *Motectorum pro festis totius anni Lib. Primus 4v*, Venice, Vincenti.
Reprint of *Motectorum pro festis* . . ., Nürnberg, Kauffmann.
One madrigal in Bodenschatz, *Florilegium selectissimarum cantionum*, Leipzig, Lamberg.
Three motets in *Melodiae sacrae*, Krakow, Lazari and Skalski.

1605 Reprint of *Il 5° libro de Madrigali a 5*, Venice, Gardano.
Reprint of *Il 4° libro de Madrigali a 6*, Venice, Gardano.
Reprint of *Il 8° libro de Madrigali a 5*, Venice, Gardano.
Reprint of *Il 1° libro de Villanelle a 3*, Venice, Vincenti and Amadino.
Eighteen madrigals in *Nervi d'Orfeo*, Leiden, Haestens.
Two madrigals in *Della nova Metamorfosi de diversi autori*, Milan, Tradate.

1606 Reprint of *Il 2° libro de Madrigali a 5*, Venice, Gardano.
Ten madrigals in *Hortus Musicalis*, Pavia, Nenninger.
Aussug aus L. Marentii 4 theilen, Nürnberg, Kauffmann.

1607 Reprint of *Il 4° libro de Madrigali a 5*, Venice, Gardano and Fratelli.
Reprint of *Motectorum pro festis totius anni*, Phalèse.
One madrigal in *Canzonette alla Romana*, Antwerp, Phalèse.
Three madrigals in *J. J. Gastoldi u. anderer Autorn Tricinia*, Nürnberg, Kauffmann.
One madrigal arrangement in Schmidt *Tabulatur Buch*, Strasbourg, Zetzner.
One madrigal in *Musica tolta da i madrigali di Claudio Monteverde e d'altri autori*, Milan, Tradate.

1608 Reprint of *Il 2° libro de Madrigali a 5*, Venice, Raveri.
Madrigalia 6v. . . . *in uno volumine conjunctim*, Nürnberg, Kauffmann.
Reprint of *Motectorum pro festis*. . . ., Venice, Scotto.
One madrigal in *Newe Teutsche Canzonetten*, Frankfurt-am-Main, Richter.
Reprint of *Il 9° libro de Madrigali a 5*, Venice, Raveri.

1609 Reprint of *Il 7° libro de Madrigali a 5*, Venice, Gardano.
Reprint of *Il 6° libro de Madrigali a 6*, Venice, Gardano.
Reprint of *Il 9° libro de Madrigali a 5*, Venice, Raveri.
Reprint of *Il 9° libro de Madrigali a 5*, Scotto.
Reprint of *Il 1, 2, 3, 4 e 5 lib. de Madrigali ridotti in un corpo*, Antwerp, Phalèse.

Il 6, 7, 8 et 9 lib., il suo testamento de Madrigali a 6, in un corpo ridotti, Antwerp, Phalèse.
Nine madrigals in *Hortus Musicalis Liber II*, Munich, Berg.
Four madrigals in *Hortus Musicalis, Liber tertius*, Munich, Berg.

1610   Reprint of *Il 5° libro de Madrigali a 6*, Venice, Gardano.
Collected edition of *Il 1, 2, 3, 4 et 5 libro de Madrigali a 6*, Antwerp, Phalèse.
Reprint of *Il 6° libro de Madrigali a 6*, Antwerp, Phalèse.
Reprint of *Madrigali Spirituali*, Antwerp, Phalèse.
Collected edition of *Madrigali Spirituali e Temporali a 5, 6, 8, 9 e 10*, Nürnberg, Kauffmann.
Collected edition of *Il 1, 2, 3, 4 e 5 lib. delle Villanelle*, Antwerp, Phalèse.
One madrigal in *Fatiche Spirituali*, Venice, Amadino.
Seven madrigals in *Fatiche Spirituali Libro secondo*, Venice, Amadino.
Two pieces in *Nova Metamorfosi*, Milan, Melchiorre herede di Tradate.

1611   Two motets in Schadeus, *Promptuarii* (v. 1612) *Musici*, Strasbourg, Kieffer.

1612   One madrigal in *Triumphi di Dori oder Dorothea*, Nürnberg, Kauffmann.
One motet in Schadeus, *Promptuarii musica . . . pars altera*, Strasbourg, Kieffer.
Six madrigals in *Delitiae musicae*, Utrecht, Roy and Rhenen.
One madrigal in *Musicalische Streitkräntzelein*, Nürnberg, Wagenmann.

1613   One madrigal in *Musicalisches Streitkräntzeleins*, Nürnberg, Scherff.

1614   Reprint of *Il 6° libro de Madrigali a 5*, Venice, Gardano.
Motetti a 12 (lost).
One motet in Constantino, *Selectae cantiones*, Rome, Zannetti.

1615   One motet in Gabrieli et Hassler, *Reliquiae sacrorum*, Nürnberg, Kauffmann.
One motet in *Musica vaga et artificiosa*, Venice, Vincenti.

1616   *Sacrae cantiones 5–7v.*, Venice, Amadino and Vincenti.
Five madrigals in *Madrigali de Diversi Auttori*, Loano, Castello.

1617   One motet in *Promptuarii musici . . . pars quarta*, Strasbourg, Bertram.
Three pieces arranged by Woltz in *Nova musices organicae Tablatura*, Basel, Genath.

1618   One motet in Bodenschatz, *Florilegium Portense*, Leipzig, Lamberg and Closemann.

1619   Two madrigals in *Triumphi de Dorothea*, Leipzig, Köber.

1621   One motet in Constantino, *Sacrae cantiones*, Antwerp, Phalèse.
Two motets in Bodenschatz, *Florilegii Musici Portensis, pars altera*, Leipzig, Lamberg.

1622   One motet in Donfried, *Promptuarii musici . . .*, Strasbourg, Ledertz.

1623   One motet in Donfried, *Promptuarii musici . . . pars altera*, Strasbourg, Ledertz.

1624   Three madrigals in *Erster Theil lieblicher, welscher Madrigalien*, Nürnberg, Halbmayer.
Two madrigals in *D.O.M.A. Exercitatio Musica*, Magdeburg, Dillinger.

1627   Four madrigals in *Extract oder erster Theil auss dem musicalischen Interim Ambrosii Profii*, Wittenberg, Gorman.

1632   Reprint of *Il 6, 7, 8 et 9 lib., il suo testamento de Madrigali a 6*, Antwerp, Phalèse.
Thirty-three villanelle in *Fiore de Villanelle*, Treviso, Righettini.